EXPECT THE MIRACLE

OF CONVERSION

7 Keys to Bringing Souls
unto Christ

EXPECT THE MIRACLE
OF CONVERSION

7 Keys to Bringing Souls
unto Christ

HARTMAN RECTOR, JR.

iv

ISBN: 1-55517-258-X

1 2 3 4 5 6 7 8 9 10

Published and Distributed by:

925 North Main, Springville, UT 84663 • 801/489-4084

CFI | Publishing and Distribution Since 1986

Cedar Fort, Incorporated

CFI Distribution • CFI Books • Council Press • Bonneville Books

Cover Design by Lyle Mortimer
Page Layout and Design by Tosha Baker and Rene A. Muñoz
Edited by Lisa Williams
Printed in the United States of America

Table of Contents

Preface

A conversion to the gospel of Jesus Christ is a real miracle. To take the "natural man" who is self-centered and selfish, headstrong, impatient, miserable, and totally set on having his own way and to make him as a child—submissive, meek, humble, patient, full of love and willing to submit to all things which the Lord sees fit to inflict upon him even as a child doth submit to his father (parents)—is truly a miraculous accomplishment. If this change does not take place, there is no way that man (also meaning women and children who have reached the years of accountability) can possibly be happy—not in this life or in the eternities to come. Happiness is only possible when man is at peace with himself, his fellowman and his God.

Of course, the Lord is totally responsible for happiness. When we keep His commandments, the Lord gives us a good or happy feeling. If we do not keep His commandments, we are not obeying Him, which means we are serving the Devil. Since we receive our blessings "from him whom we listeth to obey" (see Alma 3:26-27, D&C 29:45), and we are obeying the Devil who doesn't own anything, then we can receive no blessings. All blessings come from above (the Lord) (see D&C 130: 20-21). So in order to be blessed, we must obey the Lord, which means we must keep His commandments—all of which are totally calculated to make us happy. When we keep the commandments, we draw near unto the Lord and He then draws near unto us, or as Malachi recorded the words of the Lord, "Return unto me, and I will return unto you" (Malachi 3:7). We "return unto the Lord" by keeping his commandments.

The first commandment of happiness with which one must comply is, "Repent ye, repent ye, and be baptized in the name of my Beloved Son" (2 Nephi 31:11). And then is added to this, "He that endureth to the end, the same shall be saved" (2 Nephi 31:15). Enduring to the end means, among other things: 1), continuing to repent for the rest of our lives; 2), continuing to forgive others for the rest of our lives; and 3), being nice, or in other words, having charity which means we must love and serve our fellowman. Charity is known as the "pure love of Christ" (Moroni 7:47). Jesus Christ is the epitome of charity, or love plus sacrifice. While hanging on the cross, He could even ask His Father to forgive those who crucified Him. Charity is so vitally important because "it never fails" to produce positive results. Therefore, it becomes the foundation of all effective service which is rendered to our fellow beings and thus to God. (It is true that if we are not serving our fellow beings we are not serving God).

Jesus said, "If ye have not charity, ye are nothing." Charity then, or love plus sacrifice, is the key to bringing souls unto God. It is a fact that almost no one can turn down love. Love is the magic that makes all good things happen. When we effectively implement love plus sacrifice into our lives, then we can expect the miracle of conversion as we labor to bring souls unto Christ. But how do we effectively implement charity in our lives?

This book outlines the principles that govern both the gift of charity and the miracle of conversion. These principles of conversion are grounded in the scriptures, predicated on eternal law. As we implement these principles in our lives, we become more effective missionaries and more converted members. In essence, we prepare ourselves to embark in the service of God.

"For behold the field is white already to harvest; and lo, he that thrusteth in his sickle with his might, the same layeth up in store that he perisheth not, but bringeth salvation to his soul" (D&C 4:4).

CHAPTER ONE

Understanding
How Christ Saves

The gospel is very simple—once we have sufficient faith in the Lord Jesus Christ that we believe He has paid for our sins, then we will repent. Nobody repents until he/she believes in Christ. Therefore, it is absolutely necessary to preach Christ to the sinner (which happens to be all mankind). When I say "preach Christ," I mean teach the truth about Jesus Christ, the only begotten of God the Father in the flesh, and the firstborn in the spirit. Jesus Christ is unique among those born of mortal woman in the flesh. From his immortal Father, He inherited power over sin and power over death. From his mortal mother, Mary, He inherited power to lay down His life, or in other words, He could die. But from his immortal Father, He had power to take His body up again. Christ said, "No man taketh it [my life] from me, but I lay it down of myself. I have power to lay it down and I have power to take it again" (John 10: 17-18), which He did on the third day after the crucifixion. After He died, He then broke that band of death and made the resurrection a reality for all mankind—"for as in Adam all die, even so in Christ shall all be made alive" (1 Cor. 15:22).

The resurrection is a free gift for all by the grace of Jesus Christ. It is not necessary for mankind to do anything to receive this gift. Everyone is going to live again whether they want to or not. In fact, there will be a lot of people who will be resurrected who won't want to be.

Why wouldn't they want to be resurrected? Because they will not be in condition to receive a glorious resurrection. They will not have been cleansed of their sins; therefore, they will not be able to return and live with their Heavenly Parents (See D&C 84: 74). This is because in the resurrection they will be "filthy still" (see 2 Nephi 9:13-16, 23-24, Moroni 9:13,14). As members and missionaries of the Church of Jesus Christ of Latter-day Saints, it is necessary for us to make known the truth about Jesus Christ and His sacrifice for our sins to every nation, kindred, tongue, and people (see Matt. 24:14, D&C 88-103).

Because Christ received power over sin in His conception from His immortal Father, not only could He live without sin, but He could also pay for our sins on condition of *our* repentance (see D&C 18: 10-12). This He did in the Garden of Gethsemane and on the cross of Calvary. However, this is not a free gift as is resurrection. It comes only to those who repent of their sins and follow Him down into the waters of baptism and then come forth and receive the Holy Ghost by the laying on of hands of those who have authority from Jesus Christ to perform the saving ordinances of the gospel.

It is a fact that there is a great difference between stopping sinning and repentance. There are many people who stop committing certain sins all the time. They stop for a variety of reasons. For example, they are afraid they might get AIDS, or they might die of lung cancer, or heart disease, etc. But the problem is they are still guilty. They have not been cleansed of their sins. Only Jesus Christ can cleanse us of our sins (see 2 Nephi 25:20, 31:21, Mosiah 3:19), and He cleanses us only if we confess them and forsake them and follow Him down unto the waters of baptism and then come forth and receive the Holy Ghost in His designated way. It is a fact that salvation is only in Christ, and it must be done in His own way (see Mosiah 3:17). This is the message that His servants carry to the nations of the earth. It doesn't make much difference what man *thinks* about it. It is what God *thinks* that is all important!

The truth about Jesus Christ and the true doctrines of Christ must be carried to all God's children by the missionaries who are the Lord's special witnesses whom He sends to the nations of the earth. Although the true doctrines of Christ are in the Book of Mormon, having been restored therein after being lost from the Bible (see 1 Nephi 13:40), they still must be preached and explained by the missionaries. This is true primarily because faith in Jesus Christ comes from hearing the word of God (See Romans 10:17), not from just reading the word of God. In the words of Paul, "For whosoever shall call upon the name of the Lord shall be saved. How shall they call upon Him in whom they have not believed? And how shall they believe in Him of whom they have not heard? And how shall they hear without a preacher, and how shall they preach except they be "sent" (Romans 10: 13-15)–"sent" meaning called, ordained, set apart, and sent forth to bring the true doctrines of Jesus Christ to every nation, kindred, tongue, and people where they are permitted to go.

If it was possible to become converted to Jesus Christ by just reading the Book of Mormon, then the most economical approach to bringing people to Christ would be to send a copy of the Book of Mormon to everyone and pay them five dollars to read it. If they would not read it for

five dollars, we could up the ante to ten or fifteen or twenty-five or one hundred dollars. We could go up to three
thousand five hundred dollars to get the book read if that
was all that was necessary to bring people to Christ, and
still it would be cheaper than it is today to bring a convert
into the Church. But it takes more than reading. As Paul
testified, faith in Jesus Christ comes from hearing the true
doctrines of Christ preached by His authorized servants.
That is how important our missionaries are. They also perform a vital role in committing the non-members and less
active members to live the commandments and do the
things necessary to gain a testimony that Jesus is the Christ
and that He has restored His true Church to the earth
through living prophets in almost modern times.

Once we have faith in Jesus Christ and follow Him
into the waters of baptism and come forth and are confirmed a member of the Church of Jesus Christ of Latter-
day Saints and have received the Holy Ghost and can
speak with a new tongue, then all that is necessary is to
"endure to the end" (see 2 Nephi 31:15, Matt. 24:13).
What does "endure to the end" mean? We have discussed this briefly before in the preface but perhaps a little more in-depth discussion here might be profitable.

First: We must continue to repent for the rest of our
lives. Why? Because we will continue to make mistakes.
Not necessarily the same mistakes that we made in the
past for which we have repented, but there are so very
many ways we can commit sin, even so many that King
Benjamin said he could not number them —"but this
much I can tell you, if you do not watch yourselves, and
your thoughts and your words and your deeds and
observe the commandments of God, and continue in

faith of what ye have heard concerning the coming of our Lord, even unto the end of your lives, ye must perish, and now oh man, remember, and perish not" (Mos. 4:29-30). The way we "remember and perish not" is to continue to repent which means to confess, forsake, and partake of the sacrament which renews our baptismal covenant and makes us clean.

Second: We must continue to forgive others. It is a fact that if someone trespasses against us and we do not forgive them, we are worse than they are "for there remaineth in us the greater sin" (see D&C 64:9). So sayeth the Lord. Therefore we must forgive all men, women, and children or we cannot be forgiven ourselves. This goes along with the Master's admonition to "judge not that ye be not judged, for as ye judge ye shall be judged again" (Matt. 7:1, Luke 6:37) and Paul's admonition to "be kind one to another, tenderhearted, forgiving one another, even as God for Christ's sake hath forgiven you" (Eph. 4:32).

Three: We must be nice—meaning we must have charity, which is the pure love of Christ, or love plus sacrifice (Moroni 7:47). This means that we must take care of the poor, the needy, the downtrodden, the oppressed, and not only those who have not heard the message of the restoration, but also those who have heard but have "fallen away" and need to be reclaimed. In short, this is how we retain a remission of our sins from day to day (see Mosiah 4:26). We have already considered how we gain a remission of our sins. Now we are considering how we *retain* what we have gained. This has to do with rendering service to our fellow beings.

This is in perfect harmony with the Master's words in

the 24th chapter of Matthew where he tells us "inasmuch as ye have done it unto one of the least of these, my brethren, ye have done it unto me," and conversely inasmuch as ye did it not to one of the least of these, ye did it not unto me. Then he adds: "These shall go away unto everlasting punishment, but the righteous (those who have charity and reach out to the needy or who really are "nice") shall go unto life eternal" (see Matt. 24:31-46).

It is vital that we seek this charity and seek for opportunities to serve our fellow men, women and children or we cannot be called "the children of God." In essence, we cannot be happy. This is the first step in the successful conversion of ourselves and our fellow beings.

CHAPTER TWO

Preaching with Love

We are living today upon an earth that is dark. Perhaps just before the time of the flood was an even more difficult time to live than is today, but not much. We know that prior to the coming of the Master in his glory, the conditions will be almost exactly as they were at the time of the flood. In his own words, the Master said, "As it was in the days of Noah, so it shall be also at the coming of the Son of Man" (JS-Matt. 1:41). So living here upon the earth in this day and time is a very trying, difficult experience. Obviously the Lord would see fit to reserve those who had ability to withstand such temptation for this particular time. I don't think that you are here by accident. The Prophet Joseph Smith said, "Every man who has a calling to minister to the inhabitants of the world was ordained to that very purpose in the Grand Council of heaven before the world was" (Teachings of the Prophet Joseph Smith, p. 365).

There is a design in your being here. The prophet Alma essentially said the same thing. He was talking about the ordination of certain priests, and he said:

> And those priests were ordained after the order of his Son, in a manner that thereby the people might know in what manner to look forward to his Son for redemption.
> And this is the manner after which they were ordained—being called and prepared from the foundation of the world according to the foreknowledge of God, on account of their exceeding faith and good works (Alma 13: 2-3).

Those priests were called because of their exceeding faith and good works. I've had a number of young men that were called and ordained and set apart and sent to me (as a mission president), and I am quite sure it wasn't anything they had done since they were born that got them ordained. It's who they were before they were born and the foreknowledge of God. They didn't know what they could do, but after they arrived in the mission field they were powerful. They found that they could do all things.

> Called and prepared from the foundation of the world according to the foreknowledge of God, on account of their exceeding faith and good works; in the first place being left to choose good or evil; therefore they having chosen good, and exercising exceedingly great faith, are called with a holy calling. . . .
>
> And thus they have been called to this holy calling on account of their faith, while others would reject the Spirit of God on account of the hardness of their hearts and blindness of their minds, while, if it had not been for this they might have had a great privilege as their brethren.
>
> Or in fine, in the first place they were on the same standing with their brethren; this holy calling being prepared from the foundation of the world for such as would not harden their hearts, being in and through the atonement of the Only Begotten Son.
>
> And thus being called by this holy calling, and ordained unto the high priesthood of the holy order of God, to teach his commandments unto the children of men, that they also might enter into his rest (Alma 13: 6).

All of this calling and ordaining has been done so

that we can teach the commandments of God to the children of men. That was said in ancient times. However, President Spencer W. Kimball said essentially the same thing in modern times as recorded in the Ensign, May 1979.

> Now, my brothers and sisters, it seems clear to me, indeed this impression weighs upon me, that the Church is at a point in its growth and development when we are at last ready to move forward in a major way.

The Lord through his Prophet, in talking about the Church, was talking about you and me. We are the Church. He literally is saying that we are going to do something great and tremendous. Wouldn't you like to know what you are going to do? Well, he tells you:

> We have paused on some plateaus long enough. Let us resume our journey forward and upward. Let us quietly put an end to our reluctance to reach out to others.

Would you say that is your problem? Are you reluctant to reach out to others? In order to serve your fellowman, you have to love them. It is vitally important that you love people if you are really going to serve them. Otherwise, they will not allow you to serve them. Love is the basis of the gospel of Jesus Christ, and I submit that it is the basis of our lives.

So the commandment is very plain to us. Do you remember when the Master had washed his apostles' feet the night before He was nailed on the cross? He said to them:

A new commandment, I give unto you, That ye
love one another; as I have loved you, that ye also
love one another.

By this shall all men know that ye are my disciples, if ye have love one to another (John 13:34-35).

The Master called this a new commandment, but
there is nothing new about it. It is the law of Moses. But
it is new and everlasting in its application (as is the new
and everlasting covenant of marriage. It is new to you
when you receive it, although it is everlasting in that it
has always existed with God). To those apostles, it was a
rather new commandment, I think. I could see how they
would take very unkindly the crucifixion of their Master.
We know how Peter felt. He drew his sword and cut off
the high priest's servant's ear. Now I don't know
whether he was just a poor swordsman, or whether he
was trying to make a point. The Master said, "Put up
again thy sword unto his place: for all they that take the
sword shall perish with the sword" (Matthew 26:52).
Then He restored the ear. Then in an object lesson for all,
as He hung on the cross, He said, "Father, forgive them;
for they know not what they do" (Luke 23:24).

You have to love people to do that. If the apostles had
gone out the next day to get even, with revenge and vin-
dictiveness in their hearts, I submit to you that the gospel
of Jesus Christ would never have "gotten off the ground."
It would have died, too, in 1847 when the Saints were
being driven out of the continental limits of the United
States out to a desert valley. They could have said, "Okay
that's enough. We've done all we're going to do for you.
You can go your own way now." But as you know, one of

the very first things they did was turn around and send missionaries right back to those who had driven them out. Because they forgave, the gospel of Jesus Christ is once again founded on a bedrock foundation here in the Salt Lake Valley, and from this place we have been able to send missionaries through all the world, in fact, to every kindred tongue and people where we are permitted to go. So these Saints were great not only because they were stalwart or had an all encompassing desire to persist or persevere and to prevail, but they were great because of their Christ-like attitude of forgiveness. Their trust was first in the Lord, and then in themselves, and they were in very deed the children of God.

The gospel must go forth, but it must be preached with love. Only if we can love people will they listen to us. Some people are not easy to love. But the Savior said, "Love your enemies. Do good to those that despitefully use you. Turn the other cheek. Go the second mile." That's not easy. In fact, it is very difficult. It is easy to love people who love you, isn't it? Right away you know that they must have excellent judgment. But you don't really get credit from the Lord, I believe, for only loving people that love you unless you can love people that not only don't love you, but don't even like you. Only then will you be like your Father in Heaven, (or that much like Him anyway), who lets his rain fall on the just *and* the unjust.

You must love all people. But you have to be awfully good to love people that don't love you. How do you suppose you could get that good—that you could love people whether they love you or whether they don't? I wondered about that for a long time. I wondered about that before I ever heard of the Mormons, as a matter of fact. I was talking with my aunt one time about this particular thing. Why does God loves us? Maybe if we could find out, we would know how to love others.

There are a lot of reasons why God could love us. We are His children. Generally speaking, you love what's yours, don't you? But that's awfully selfish, don't you think? I don't think God loves us because we are His children, though we are. I think He would love us if we belonged to someone else. Maybe He loves us because we are good. You sure hope not, don't you? That is the last thing in the world we want. No, He doesn't love us because we are good, though I am sure He is more pleased with us when we are good. I believe that because I find that I am more pleased with my own children when they keep my commandments. If they don't keep my commandments, they could get spanked. If you don't keep the Lord's commandments, I promise you you'll get spanked. "Whom the Lord loveth, he chasteneth and scourgeth every son" (Hebrews 12:6). The fact that we get spanked doesn't mean we aren't loved.

Maybe God loves us because of our potential. It is easy to love people that have a lot of potential. We all have heroes. I find I really love Abe Lincoln. I love the Prophet Joseph Smith. But if the Lord loves us because of our potential, and some people seem to have more than others, does that mean God loves you more than He loves me? He said He doesn't. "And the one being is as precious in his sight as the other" (Jacob 2:21).

God doesn't love us because of our potential. He doesn't love us because we are good. He doesn't love us because we're His. Well, why on earth does He love us then? My good aunt told me the answer to this question when I was a small boy. She said, "Junior, God doesn't love us because we are good; He loves us because *He* is good." And I knew that was true. When you hear the truth, you recognize it. Yes, He is all good, and so He loves us. He'd almost have to be all good to love us, wouldn't He?

So how do we also get that way? How do we become so good that we can love people whether they deserve it or whether they don't? I found the answer in the Book of Mormon. It is in Mosiah Chapter 2 verse 4. King Benjamin was talking to his people, and he said that he taught them "to keep the commandments of God, that they might rejoice and be filled with love towards God and all men." The commandments are calculated to make you so good that you can love people whether they deserve it or whether they don't! So our first responsibility, in order to serve, is to keep the commandments of God ourselves. Keep the commandments precisely. I promise you it will turn you into a loving, serving son or daughter of our Heavenly Father. The Master said, "I am among you as he that serveth" (Luke 22: 27). The Master gave His life as a ransom for many. It is love plus sacrifice, which I would interpret to mean charity, that really permits us to render service. It is difficult, of course, but you will find it through obedience to His commandments. I don't think you will find it any other way.

A young man taught me this principle very forcibly over 16 years ago. I was serving as a mission president in San Diego. I got a call from the Missionary Department one day and they said they had a young man over in Thailand who had been there for nine months. He had learned the language fluently, but he had quit and come home because he hadn't had a baptism. They had asked him to stop and talk with me on the way home. He wanted to go home so badly that he was willing to do that. So he came into my office, and there he sat, a handsome, good-looking, obviously smart young man. He had learned the language and could speak it fluently. I said, "Elder, how on earth could you spend nine months in Thailand, learn the language fluently, and not baptize anybody? All you would have to do is walk out on the streets of Bangkok and say, 'Excuse me, I'm a Mormon Elder. I have authority to baptize. Would you like to be baptized?' That's really all you have to do is ask people. I'm sure you would have baptized somebody in nine months, speaking the language the way you do. I know it works that way."

It worked that way for a young man in Frankfurt, Germany who had been there for a year and hadn't had a baptism. He was very distressed; he wanted to go home. I had an interview with him. We went over the handbook to see if there might be a few things he should be doing that he wasn't doing and a few things he shouldn't be doing that he was doing, and we found a few things in both categories. He committed himself to follow the mission rules, and to live God's commandments with exactness.

I said, "The only other thing you have to do, Elder, is just promise me that one day a week you'll get out on the streets in Frankfurt, (and I recommend that you pick a nice shopping center where there are lots of people) and don't let anybody pass you that day without saying, 'Excuse me, I'm a Mormon Elder. I have authority to baptize. Would you like to be baptized? Before I see you again, you'll have a baptism. I promise.'"

He said, "I'll do it!"

I saw him six months later and he had five baptisms. I said, "Elder, how did you get your contacts?" "I just asked people if they wanted to be baptized." I told that to a ward mission leader up in Carlsbad, California. Two weeks later he baptized his very best friend—a lifelong, childhood friend. I asked, "How did you do it?"

He answered, "I said to him, 'I'm a Mormon Elder. I have authority to baptize. Would you like to be baptized?'"

His friend said, "Yes, I really would, but is there something else I have to do first?"

He said, "Yeah, I have to teach you a little bit." Two weeks later he baptized his best friend. That's what it takes. You have to ask people.

The young man from Bangkok said, "President Rector, I don't like those people. I don't like the way they look. I don't like the way they act. I don't like the way they smell. They are arrogant." And he knew about arrogance.

I said, "Well, Elder, I understand why you haven't baptized anybody. You have to love people in order to baptize them. Why don't you let me send you up to Carlsbad, California? We're having a little success up there with the Spanish-speaking people. I'm sure that you could love them enough to bring them into the Church. I know you don't speak Spanish. We could send you down to Provo, Utah to the Missionary Training Center for two months where you would learn to speak the language fluently. But there's no sense in doing that. I can send you up to Carlsbad, and you can get on-the-job-training."

He said he didn't want to go. I said, "What difference does that make? How many times on this earth do you have to do things that you don't want to do? Isn't that what life is really all about, doing a bunch of things that you don't particularly want to do? I don't suppose that Abraham wanted to offer his son as a burnt sacrifice, do you? I don't think the Master wanted to die on the cross, either. If He did, He was acting very strangely in the Garden of Gethsemane the night before it happened. And I know for sure that Jonah did not want to go on a mission."

But life is all about doing things you don't want to do. My father taught me the importance of this lesson. He hoodwinked me into milking our cows. He said to me one time, "You're not old enough, nor big enough to milk." And I knew I was. I was seven years old–of course I was big enough to milk. And so I proved to him that I could milk. I could make the foam stand high on the bucket. My father said, "I believe you can milk. You've got the job." And for the next twelve years I milked from eight to twelve cows night and morning. I decided I did not want to milk. I said that to him one time. "Dad, I don't want to milk." He said, "That's okay. You don't have to want to as long as you do it." That's kind of how the Lord treats us. It's the doing that makes the difference.

I gave the Elder from Bangkok a blessing and promised him he would have baptisms, at least two in two months. He left for Carlsbad and almost came home after his first month. But he had committed himself to stay. He had learned that if you are going to serve the Lord, you are going to have to commit yourself to do so. It's like Abigail Adams said to her husband John, who was President of the United States at the time, "Do you remember what you said to me, John? You said, 'Commitment, Abby, commitment. There are only two creatures worthy to live, one who makes commitments and one who requires commitments of others.'"

The Elder was twenty-eight days into the second month and I was getting a little nervous when I got a call from him. He said, "President Rector, I baptized two people last night."

I said, "Elder, that's tremendous. Tell me about it. How did you do it?"

He said, "Well, we were teaching about twenty-five at one time. We were in our commitment lesson where we commit them to keep the commandments, pay their tithing, live the Word of Wisdom, attend church, etc. There were two in the group who couldn't make those commitments. So the Elders pulled them out and put them in a room by themselves. (They didn't want any negative influence in their commitment session). I was walking down the hall, and I saw them in the room. The Spirit told me to go in to talk to them."

("Oh that's a good sign when the Spirit starts telling you what to do.")

"I went in," the Elder said. "I pulled a chair up and sat down. One of the investigators looked remarkably like my own brother. As I sat down in that chair, I don't know what happened to me, but a feeling of love came over me. I said to the one, 'I really do love you.' The tears rolled down my cheeks and his cheeks, too. A short time later, I baptized him. Then I baptized his friend."

In the next six months, that young Elder baptized 350 Spanish-speaking people. I transferred him down to San Diego where we also had Spanish-speaking people. I made him a district leader. He and his companion were walking down the street one day and saw some Thai writing on the window of a building. The Elder from Bangkok went in and spoke Thai with the proprietor. The proprietor was very surprised because the Elder didn't look like a Thai. The Elder called me very excited and said, "President Rector, did you know that there are fifty Thai families that live here in my area?"

I said, "You don't mean it?"

He said, "Yes, they're here. Can I teach them?"

I said, "Now, Elder, let's think about it for a minute. If you teach them, you'll have to be their fellowshippers, too. They have to go to Church. They won't understand anything in English so you will have to translate everything for them. Are you willing to be their fellowshipper as well as their proselytizer?"

"Yes, yes, I'll do it," he said.

I said, "Okay, let's see what you can do."

Three weeks later he called me and said, "President Rector, I just baptized the most beautiful family of five you have ever seen—a father and a mother and three children, all Thai. They don't speak a word of English."

I said, "Elder, that's wonderful. Tell me about those people, will you? What kind of people are they anyway?"

He said, "Oh they are the sweetest people. They are so nice and humble. They are just like the Mexicans," (or the Japanese, or the Germans, or anyone else who comes to this particular point of conversion).

I said, "Tell me, Elder, how do they smell?"

He said, "Yeah, that's right. It's me. I'm the one that's changed."

When we change, everyone around us changes, too. Do you remember what the Master said? In Matthew 25, he said:

> When the son of Man shall come in his glory, and all the holy angels with him, then shall he sit upon the throne of his glory:
>
> And before him shall be gathered all nations: and he shall separate them one from another, as a shepherd divideth his sheep from the goats:
>
> And he shall set the sheep on his right hand, but the goats on the left.
>
> Then shall the King say unto them on his right hand, Come, ye blessed of my Father, inherit the Kingdom prepared for you from the foundation of the world:
>
> For I was an hungered, and ye gave me meat: I was thirsty, and ye gave me drink: I was a stranger, and ye took me in:
>
> Naked, and ye clothed me: I was sick, and ye visited me: I was in prison, and ye came unto me.
>
> Then shall the righteous answer him saying, Lord, when saw we thee an hungered, and fed thee? or thirsty, and gave thee drink:
>
> When saw we thee a stranger, and took thee in? or naked, and clothed thee?
>
> Or when saw we thee sick, or in prison, and came unto thee? (Matt: 25: 31-39).

I can almost hear them say "I don't ever remember seeing you like this. Are you sure it was me? People do look a lot alike you know. You must have mistaken me for someone else."

Have you ever been given credit for something good that you didn't do? How does that make you feel? Not all that great. Sometimes we *will* let people give us credit for something good that we didn't do, but we never, ever would let anybody give us credit for something bad that we didn't do. That's kind of the way we all are, isn't it? We are all pretty much alike.

> And the King shall answer and say unto them, Verily I say unto you,
> Inasmuch as ye have done it unto one of the least of these my brethren, ye have done it unto me.
> Then shall he say also unto them on the left hand, Depart from me, ye cursed, into everlasting fire, prepared for the devil and his angels:
> For I was an hungered, and ye gave me no meat. . . .
> Then shall they also answer him, saying, Lord, when saw we thee an hungered. . . and did not minister unto thee?
> Then shall he answer them, saying, Verily I say unto you, Inasmuch as ye did it *not* to one of the least of these, ye did it not to me (Matt. 25: 40, 42, 44-45).

I presume that is how the judgment will really be. It will have to do with whether or not you really serve your fellowman. For John "saw the dead, small and great stand before God and the books were opened and another book was opened which was the book of life. And the dead were judged out of those things that were written in the books according to their works" (Rev. 20:12). That's what it all comes down to. If we love people, we can serve them. If we don't, we can't, because they won't let us.

The secret to love is obedience to the commandments of God. Keep the commandments and I promise you will rejoice and be filled with love towards God and all men.

CHAPTER THREE

Inviting all to Come Unto Christ

The mission of the Church is to invite all to come unto Christ and be perfected in Him (see Moroni 10:32). The mission of the church hinges on the principle of love. First, we are to preach the gospel to every nation, kindred, tongue, and people; second, we must redeem the dead; and third, we must perfect the Saints. Missionary work comes first. It has always come first. It has to be first. It was the first responsibility laid upon the Church in this dispensation and it is a responsibility that has never been rescinded, nor will it ever be.

President Kimball said missionary work is the bedrock foundation of the Church. The convert is the lifeblood of the church. If there were no converts, the church would shrivel and die on the vine. I heard him say that many times. The last time I heard him say it, he added, "and blow away." We would lose the kingdom of God from the earth if we didn't have converts. We must continue to bring souls to the Lord. The Savior died so that all men could come unto Him. This doctrine is stated plainly in the Book of Mormon in Third Nephi, chapter 27, verse 13:

> Behold I have given unto you my gospel, and this is the gospel which I have given unto you, that I came into the world to do the will of my Father, because my Father sent me.

The Savior came to do the will of His Father because

He was sent here by the Father. He did not come to do his "own thing," nor did he come to "feather his own nest." I do not presume He really wanted to die on the cross. In the Garden of Gethsemane the night before it happened, he said, "If it can be, Father, let this cup pass from me. Nevertheless, not as I will, but as Thou wilt" (Matt. 26:39). The Savior came to do the will of the Father, and you and I, who are going to serve the Lord, must do the will of the Father. We must do the will of He that sent us, the same as Jesus had to do the will of He that sent Him. And what did His Father send him to do? "And my Father sent me that I might be lifted up upon the cross" (3 Nephi 27:14). The Savior came to die, to give his life as a ransom for many. "No man taketh it (my life) from me," He said, "I lay it down of myself." He did precisely that. "My Father sent me that I might be lifted up upon the cross and after that I had been lifted up upon the cross, that I might draw all men unto me" (John 10:18). The Redeemer was lifted up to draw all men unto Him. "That as I have been lifted up by men even so should men be lifted up by the Father, to stand before me, to be judged of their works, whether they be good or whether they be evil" (3 Nephi 27:14).

Why are we resurrected? So we can be judged according to our works. We will be judged on the basis of deeds done in the flesh (see Alma 5:15). We will not be judged on what happened before we came to this earth nor are we judged on what happens after we die. We will be judged on what happens while we are here, judged according to the deeds done in the flesh. That is the reason we are resurrected–to be judged. I presume you cannot judge a spirit. Nor, can you exalt a spirit. Exaltation comes through resurrection and righteousness.

"And it shall come to pass that whoso repenteth and is baptized in my name shall be filled" (3 Nephi 27:16). What with? The Holy Ghost, of course. You will be filled with the Holy Ghost if you repent and are baptized. "And if he endureth to the end, behold, him will I hold guiltless before my Father at that day when I shall stand to judge the world. And he that endureth not unto the end, the same is he that is also hewn down and cast into the fire, from whence they can no more return, because of the justice of the Father" (3 Nephi 27:16-17).

God is just. He is a loving God. But He is very, very just. Mercy cannot rob justice; however, mercy can satisfy the demands of justice. This is plainly taught by the great prophet Amulek in the 34th chapter of Alma.

> And behold, this is the whole meaning of the law, every whit pointing to that great and last sacrifice, and that great and last sacrifice will be the Son of God, yea, infinite and eternal.
>
> And thus he shall bring salvation to all those who shall believe on his name; this being the intent of this last sacrifice, to bring about the bowels of mercy, which overpowereth justice, and bringeth about means unto men that they may have faith unto repentance.
>
> And thus mercy can satisfy the demands of justice, and encircle them in the arms of safety, while he that exercised no faith unto repentance is exposed to the whole law of the demands of justice; therefore, only unto him that has faith unto repentance is brought about the great and eternal plan of redemption (Alma 34:14-16).

And so faith in Jesus Christ unto repentance is the key. It is a fact that no one repents until they have sufficient faith in Jesus Christ that they believe He has paid for their sins. We must bring souls to the Lord through faith and repentance. How can they believe in Him whom they have not heard, and how can they hear except there be a preacher, and how can they preach except they be sent? (see Romans 10:14-15). We need preachers to bring souls to the Lord. You see, we are sinners. We're all sinners. We desperately need a Savior, and that is who the Lord Jesus Christ is. He is our Savior. He paid the price for our sins, but that is on condition of repentance (see D&C 18:11). I did not make that up. John says every man that says he is not a sinner is a liar, and the truth is not in him (see 1 John 1:8-10). And so we need to bring souls to the Lord, but we need to bring them through faith in Him as the Savior and the Redeemer. He is the only way, our only access back to God. That is the message that we must carry to the world. Now there is a difference in stopping sinning and repentance. People stop sinning all the time, but they are still guilty. True repentance means you not only stop sinning but you follow the Lord down into the waters of baptism and then come forth and receive the Holy Ghost by one who has authority to perform these ordinances.

Of course, it's not all over when you have faith, repentance, and are baptized by water and by the Spirit. We must also endure to the end. Endurance means we continue to repent, continue to forgive, to be nice (to be charitable), and to keep the covenants we make with the Lord. Thereby we stay on a straight and narrow path. Exaltation comes as a result of living in obedience to our covenants and staying on the straight and narrow path.

> And this is the word which he hath given unto the children of men. And for this cause he fulfilleth the words which he hath given, and he lieth not, but fulfilleth all his words.
>
> And no unclean thing can enter into his kingdom; therefore nothing entereth into his rest save it be those who have washed their garments in my blood, because of their faith, and repentance of all their sins, and their faithfulness unto the end.
>
> Now this is the commandment: Repent all ye ends of the earth, and come unto me and be baptized in my name, that ye may be sanctified by the reception of the Holy Ghost, that ye may stand spotless before me at the last day. Verily, verily, I say unto you, this is my gospel (3 Nephi 27: 18-21).

And so this is the message that He would have us carry forth, and we must teach all men. Before we can do that, we must understand it ourselves. We must be filled with the Spirit which can only come as we look unto the Lord, as we experience this conversion in our own lives. Missionaries must be converted. The Spirit then becomes all important. For what happens to people who do not come unto Him? In the 84th section, verse 74, the Lord says, "Verily, verily I say unto you, they who believe not on your words, and are not baptized in water in my name, for the remission of their sins, that they may receive the Holy Ghost, shall be damned" (or, stopped in their progression). Now, no one enjoys that. Not even the devil enjoys it. Because of his disobedience, he was cast out, and so, damned, stopped in his progression. "He wants all men to be miserable like unto himself" (2 Nephi 2:27). So Nephi says, you'll never be happy in iniquity.

"Wickedness never was happiness," said Alma (Alma 41:10). Not only must we get cleaned up ourselves, but we have to help others get cleaned up, too. "And [they] shall not come into my Father's kingdom where my Father and I am. And this revelation unto you, and commandment, is in force from this very hour upon all the world, and the gospel is unto all who have not received it. But verily I say unto all those to whom the kingdom has been given . . . " (D& C 84:74, 76). And who's that? Well, that's you and me. We have the kingdom. Here we are, just a handful, yet we have the kingdom of God. Does that tell you how many you have responsibility for? How are you doing? Do you feel good about yourself?

Listen to what President Kimball prayed in a meeting with Regional Representatives. He said:

> Oh our beloved Father in Heaven, bring about the day when we may be able to bring in large numbers as Ammon and his brethren did, thousands of conversions, not tens or fives or one, thousands of conversions. The Lord promises. He fulfills His promises. Our Father, may we move forward with Jesus Christ as our advocate to establish the Church among the inhabitants of the earth. May Jacob's flock flower and flourish in the wilderness and blossom as the rose upon the mountain. May we merit the promise that the Lord will do things that we can hardly believe. May we improve the efficiency of our missionaries, each bringing thousands of converts into the Church.

Thousands each one of us, we have to do it. Is there some other way? There is no other way. Who else can?

No one else can do it. We must have faith in the Lord
Jesus Christ. We must repent of our sins, change, turn
away and make a covenant with the Lord in the waters
of baptism. Baptism is for the remission of sins and a
witness before God that we will be obedient unto Him
in keeping his commandments (see 2 Nephi 31:6). Then
we must receive the Holy Ghost by by the laying on of
hands. Then we must endure to the end.

You see, we have all proven ourselves in the spirit
world. If we had not, we wouldn't be here. Everybody
you see walking around on the street has a body of flesh
and bones. If you can see them, you know they were
faithful in the spirit world. We had to accept the plan of
salvation or we could not come to this earth. So everybody you see is "fair game." What we have to do is get
their attention and recall to their memory what they
have already accepted but have forgotten. That makes it
easy, right? All you've got to do is get their attention.
And then you have a message for them– "You proved
yourself there, now you have to prove yourself here, just
as the Lord Jesus Christ Himself had to prove Himself
here." Nephi in the 31st chapter of 2nd Nephi, verse six,
makes this very plain when he says:

> And now, I would ask of you, my beloved
> brethren, wherein the Lamb of God did fulfill all
> righteousness in being baptized by water?
> Know ye not that he was holy? But notwith-
> standing he being holy [which means he was with-
> out sin], he showeth unto the children of men that
> according to the flesh [this flesh relates to mortal
> life], he humbleth himself before the Father, and
> witnesseth unto the Father that he would be obedi-
> ent unto him in keeping his commandments.

Christ had already proven himself obedient in the spirit, and so have you, and so has everybody you see. But you have to prove yourself again, in the flesh. Even the Lord Jesus Christ had to prove Himself in the flesh. And so, everyone must prove themselves in the flesh.

Faith, repentance, baptism by immersion for the remission of sins, a witness before God that we will be obedient unto Him in keeping His commandments in the flesh, and then cometh the Holy Ghost by the laying on of hands. Baptism of fire and the Holy Ghost is what we are really after. The Holy Ghost is real and He works like this. If I should give you my pen, that would belong to you. It's mine. I can give it away. If I gave you my book, that would be yours. But if I gave you my power of attorney, then everything I have would be yours if you exercised it. But if I gave you my power of attorney and you never took it to the bank, or you never exercised it, you wouldn't get anything that belongs to me. That is what happens when you receive the Holy Ghost. You get the power of attorney of the Lord, and He says if you will live for it, "all that the Father has will be thine." Jesus said, "Things that I do, ye can do, and greater things that I do, ye can do because I go to the Father" (John 14:12).

Sure, you can bring thousands of souls unto the Lord. But you've got to endure to the end yourself, too. You've got to stick it out. That is what you have to do to be saved and that is what you have to teach others about salvation.

CHAPTER FOUR

Implementing the Lord's Success Formula

God grants unto men according to their desires. So said Alma in the 29th chapter, verse four — "I know that he granteth unto men according to their desire." It is true. If you have desires to serve God, ye will be called to the work, but you must have those desires.

The scriptures are calculated to fill you with the Spirit. You can even hear the Lord's voice as you read the scriptures. You will find that in the 18th section, verse 35 of the D&C.

> For it is my voice which speaketh them unto you; for they are given by my Spirit unto you, and by my power you can read them one to another; and save it were by my power you can not have them. Wherefore, you can testify that you have heard my voice, and know my words.

It is vitally important that you feast on the scriptures if you want the spirit of the Lord. I don't think you can get it in any other way. You can be called, ordained, and set apart and sent out to bring souls to the Lord and never bring a soul to the Lord because you can't bring a soul to the Lord by yourself. It is the spirit that brings souls to the Lord. As Paul said, "I planted, Apolus watered, but God gave the increase" (1 Cor. 3:6). You must get the spirit. It is a gift from God which is bestowed on those who are in condition to receive it.

Without the spirit it is absolutely impossible, but with the spirit all things are possible.

You can do precisely what President Kimball prayed to the Lord would happen—bring thousands of souls to Christ. I know you can do it. One elder in my mission baptized twenty-four hundred and forty-two converts in twenty-two months. I had a sister from Australia who baptized a thousand and sixty-four converts in eighteen months. She spent two of those months at the Missionary Training Center learning discussions in Spanish. She also had a bad back and was in bed for three months during her mission. I had two sisters who baptized seventy marines in the month of June, 1979.

There is a little success formula that was developed in the California San Diego mission. It kind of grew on us as we went about the work. It begins like this:

1. *Believe that you can do it.* You have to believe that you can. That is what the Lord wants you to do. It is not hard to incorporate an idea like that. You start by saying, "I'll do it: *I will do* it." Now you are already on the way to making it happen. You become very, very positive. That means that you have strong belief in yourself as a representative of the Lord Jesus Christ, a special witness of His holy name. He says "all things are possible unto you" (Mark 10:27). We know it is true. If He is going to tell you to do something, do you suppose that He's not going to prepare the way? What did Nephi say? "I will go and do the things which the Lord hath commanded, for I know that the Lord giveth no commandments unto the children of men, save he shall prepare a way for them that they may accomplish the thing which he command-

ed them" (1 Nephi 3:7). Do you believe it? The Lord does
not lie. King Benjamin says, "He never doth vary from
that which he has said" (Mos. 2:22). Well, if he says it,
you know it can happen, but you are the means to bring
it to pass. You are the instrument in the hand of the Lord.
And so you must yield your heart unto Him. Forget
about home, school, a girl, a car, football, baseball, bas-
ketball. I don't care what it is, forget about it. I promise
you in the name of Lord Jesus Christ that you will lose
nothing by serving him. The Lord delights to stand
behind his servants. He says He will do it and He does.

In the first section of the Doctrine and Covenants,
verse 38, the Lord says, "What I the Lord have spoken, I
have spoken, and I excuse not myself; and though the
heavens and the earth pass away, my words shall not
pass away, but shall all be fulfilled, whether by mine
own voice or by the voice of my servants, it is the
same" (D&C 1:38). It is exactly the same. You can speak
for the Lord and the Lord will stand behind you. He
delights to do that. I have seen Him do that many
times. I had two Elders one time who were teaching a
Jewish sister. One of the Elders got a little carried away.
He was teaching the law of tithing and said, "Now sister, I promise you if you pay your tithing, the Lord will
restore unto you tenfold." She said, "Tenfold? I can add,
tenfold? I'm paying my tithing tomorrow." The Elder
got a little concerned. He called me and said,
"President, I don't know why I said that," and I said, "I
don't either." He said, "What can I do?" I said, "Pray."
But I had had enough experience with the Lord's special witnesses to know that if he really didn't know why
he said what he said that he was in good shape, because

it had come from the spirit. You can depend on what the spirit says. I said, "Don't worry about it , Elder, let the Lord take care of that. You just go find somebody else to make promises to." Within two months, this sister was making twenty-five hundred dollars a month. She was in the business of making art objects out of metal there in San Diego. Her product "caught on" in the San Diego area. She had more orders than she could possibly fill. She became the most enthusiastic tithe payer I have ever known. I could call her anytime She would quit whatever she was doing. She would come with her checkbook and show what the Lord will do for you when you give Him His tenth, and she was real specific on whose tenth it was. It was His tenth. You see, the Lord God had spoken it. He will open the windows of heaven. He will pour out blessings that there will not be room enough to receive them (see Malachi 3:10). The Lord said it again in Luke 6:38. "Give and it shall be given unto you; good measure, pressed down, and shaken together, and running over, shall men give into your bosom, For with the same measure that ye mete (give) withal it shall be measured to you again."

The Lord does stand behind His servants and He will stand behind you. That is probably one of the most exciting things that will ever happen in your life when you make promises in the name of the Lord and the Lord fulfills them and you see it come to pass right before your eyes. If you will make the promises, He delights to fulfill them. If you believe that you can, you can. Of course, you have to be called, ordained, and set apart. You have got to be authorized to speak for the Lord. Authorization is necessary, and then it is important that you feel good about yourself.

As a mission president, I could always tell how the Elders and sisters were doing. I would say, "Elder, how do you feel about yourself?" He would say, "Oh I feel great, President." I'd say, "Okay, I understand you haven't any problems with basic fundamental commandments. I presume you are not completely satisfied with your performance, though, are you?" Oh no, never satisfied with the performance, always looking for ways to improve. But you feel great about yourself because you're keeping the basic fundamental commandments, and because you are, the Lord gives you a good feeling. Now you are in condition for the Lord to use you to do anything He needs done.

You have to *feel good about yourself.* You have to have self-esteem. There is a difference between self-esteem and conceit. Conceit is the weirdest disease in all the world—it makes everybody sick except the one who has got it. But one who has self-esteem is one who is positive. Feeling good about yourself comes from the Spirit. It comes from keeping the basic commandments. Believe that you can do it.

2. Look to the Lord for your blessings. You cannot depend on members of the Church to give you referrals. Oh, that would be nice. We work on them all the time. We plead with them, we tell them, "Every member's a missionary." Have you had anybody tell you that? Well, it's true. Some are lousy, but they are missionaries, nevertheless, because one's example is never lost on those around them. Do not *depend* on members to give you your contacts. It would be great if you could, it would be great if they would. We know they can. They just will not do it, that's all. I say that after many years of experience. You don't have to depend on members when you look to the Lord because the Lord can provide them for you. I had Elders that made commitments concerning how many they were going to baptize that week. You can commit yourself if you are in condition. And if you are operating under the influence of the Spirit, you can make promises. The Lord says He will stand behind them.

This one Elder made a promise he was going to baptize five people that week. We came up to about Thursday of that week. His baptisms were set for Saturday. He had two groups he was going to baptize: a couple, and a family of three (father, mother, and one child). He felt good about it so he committed himself. When Thursday came, the couple went on vacation. They were gone. They did not bother to tell him, so he could not baptize them. He could not even get in contact with them. That is like trying to baptize a spirit. And the three—the father could not quit smoking, or was unwilling to quit smoking. So there the Elder was. They had all fallen through on him. He did not have any baptisms at all. But he knew the Lord was on his side because he was on the Lord's side. As long as you are on the Lord's side, you can depend on the Lord to be on your side. That is the only way you can depend on the Lord. You have got to be on His side. And so, the Elder reported, he went over the roster of the Sunday school class and found a family of five. Can you imagine that? A family of five who were not members of the Church, but were attending church every Sunday. "So I went over and challenged them for baptism," he said. They said, "We thought nobody would ever ask us." And isn't it amazing that somebody did? You know it is hard to get in this Church. It really is. I have seen people that would just do anything in the world to get in this church, but nobody would ask them to be baptized. And so that Saturday that Elder baptized his five. He said, "President, it is just like they fell on me from out of a tree." I said, "No, they were delivered to you by the hand of the Lord." That is how it is when you go where you should be when you should be there. Look to the Lord for your blessings.

3. *Make the sacrifice.* Sacrifice brings forth the blessings of heaven. You have got to give up all thoughts that would take your mind off of what the Lord has called you to do. If you can do that, there is no limit to what you can accomplish, for you will plug into that spiritual power source. The Lord will tell you what to say. He will tell you where to go. He will tell you how to interest the children of men. Sacrifice is the key. The Lord will not deal with you on any other basis. It is the key to controlling the powers of heaven. What seems like sacrifice to one is just normal effort to another.

We had goals in the mission field. We had minimum goals of fifty-five hours of basic proselyting: that's tracting, teaching, checking referrals, and using the family involvement program. Four basic missionary actions, fifty-five hours minimum. Those who put in fifty-five hours every now and then would baptize somebody, but not very often. I met with an Elder one day, and I said, "Now, Elder, you really could not expect the Lord to bless you when you just put in the minimums. You see, the blessings are in the second mile. That means you have to do more than is expected of you. You only put in the mini-mum--that is what you are getting paid for."

He said, "Paid, I am not getting paid."

I said, "You can breathe, can't you? Do you think you have got that coming to you or something? You can see, you can feel, you can hear, you can taste. All these things the Lord gives you free. That is for the minimum. If you want blessings from the Lord, you have got to put in something above and beyond the minimums. You must go the second mile."

Those who would put in sixty and seventy hours a week baptized every month. But there were others who put in eighty, ninety, one hundred and ten basic proselyting hours in a week. That is sixteen to eighteen hours a day of basics. And how many did they baptize? Maybe twenty-five or thirty a month, that is about one convert baptism a day. That is what it takes. I know that's what it takes because I saw it done. There is no limit to what you can do if you and the Lord believe that you can. If you look to Him for your strength and are willing to make the sacrifice, all things are possible.

4. Expect a miracle. If you do not expect a miracle, you won't recognize it when it comes. I went up to Carlsbad, California and asked the Stake President what his baptismal policy was. He said, "Well, we have a baptism every Saturday at 5:30." I said, "Is that all?" He said, "Well, that is all we need." I said, "You must not have heard President Kimball. He visited San Diego. He said to those who were assembled in front of him (it was all the leadership of the nine stakes in the San Diego area at that time), 'In California last year we had 14,227 baptisms. That is good but you should have done that many right here in the San Diego mission. 14,000 for nine stakes is not very many.'"

I figured that out. It would come out to about a hundred a month per stake. A hundred a month is twenty-five a week. And so I said, "President, if you are going to follow the prophet, we are going to have to baptize twenty-five a week in your stake. You may have a bad week so we may have to baptize fifty one week to catch up. Do you really think you can put fifty people through your baptismal font at 5:30 Saturday evening?" He laughed. But we put thirty-nine through that baptismal font one day in that stake. Thirty-nine in one day. We started at nine in the morning. We finished up about midnight. There was water about six inches deep on the floor. Can you imagine what you have to do for white clothes when you are baptizing thirty-nine people at one time? We had to carry the baptismal clothes out three times that day to dry them in the dryers of members' homes locally. Nobody wants to be baptized in wet clothes. If you don't expect a miracle, the white clothes alone will carry you out. But you can expect a miracle. One of my missionaries went one hundred and fifty-six days and had a baptism every day, sometimes thirteen and fourteen a day. Now if you are not ready for that, you will never be able to do it. Expect a miracle, and you will be ready for it because miracles come to pass when you and the Lord start working together. There is no limit to what you can do with the Lord as a companion.

We had a branch out in Colexico, California. That branch was kind of like a Spanish city in the U.S. of A. It was right next to the border, this little town of Colexico with maybe ten thousand people. They had a branch there. There were three priesthood holders in the branch. They made up the branch presidency, and two of them were inactive. They had a number of women and some girls. They were having, I think on average, about twenty in attendance at their meetings.

I got a letter from the Stake President, and he said, "President Rector, I wonder if you could help us in Colexico." He said, "You have had missionaries down there, I know, and they are doing a lot of teaching, but they just are not baptizing anybody." (There had not been a baptism in that branch for about nine months, as I recall) He said, "I wonder if you have a couple of Elders that can play the guitar and maybe sing." He said, "I believe that if we entertained these people we could get them to come back to church."

I said, "I'll send you two dancing Elders." So I called two Elders and gave them an assignment to go to Colexico and baptize priesthood. Normally we concentrate on families, but we needed priesthood in that branch or the branch was going to close. That is what the Stake President said: "We are going to close the branch if we cannot get some priesthood in it." So I sent the Elders out to baptize priesthood.

These two great missionaries made their goal sheet before they left. It began:

1. In the month of July in our companionship we are having 25 baptisms.
2. We yearn for these baptisms.
3. They are all we talk about.
4. We take maximum advantage of every moment to achieve them.

5. We put forth unheard of physical and mental exertion.
6. We are finding these people through the missionary food service and the lacing program.

When I read that, I called one of the Elders and I asked him, "Elder, what is missionary food service?"

He said, "Well, President Rector, over there the workers who work in the fields get their job every morning at 4 o'clock. Not everybody gets to work everyday." He said, "We the missionaries will be there when they get their assignments, and the ones who do not get an assignment to work that day we will invite over to the chapel, which is just walking distance, to have a religious discussion and pancakes."

I said, "Elder, you know, someone might get the idea that people are coming over just to eat pancakes."

And he said, "President, did the Master ever feed anybody that He taught?"

And I said, "Well, let's see, He fed five thousand one time, four thousand another time."

He said, "Why did He feed them?"

I said, "Okay, go ahead." The Goal sheet continued:

7. We teach them boldly, skillfully, in the spirit of love.
8. We testify with power, and challenge at the drop of a hat.
9. We conclude each day with the satisfaction that another person has been baptized.
10. When we think we are too tired, that is when we receive our second wind.
11. We blow through all obstacles that Satan puts in our path and baptize these people.

12. We are in a solemn covenant with the Lord to baptize 25 souls.
13. Right now the powers of heaven are being mobilized to bring about these conversions.
14. And how great shall be our joy with them in the kingdom of our Father.

How many do you suppose they baptized that month? Yes, twenty-five, precisely the number which they had committed with the Lord, for the Lord delivered them to them. But it was not easy. These Elders in Colexico did not think about anything but how they were going to get the message to this group of people, how they were going to get their attention. They thought about it all day long. They had "tunnel vision"—and it happened..

In order to make it happen, they decided they had to baptize a certain person, and they made a covenant they would not eat or drink until he was baptized. Forty-eight hours later, with 110 to 120 degrees temperatures, they had not eaten or drunk. Now that is a bit beyond what we recommend in the handbook. We do not recommend this kind of thing. But when the Spirit speaks, you follow the Spirit. They baptized this man. He happened to be the foreman. He was the one who decided who got work every day. And some of those that were baptized were heard to say to their friend, "Now you better stop your smoking and drinking and you better start listening to the missionaries. I have had work every day since I joined this Church."

I went over when I found out what had happened to see what was transpiring in Colexico. I was called upon to speak, of course, and you might guess what I spoke on. I spoke on tithing, fast offerings, the ten command-ments and moral cleanliness. At the end of that meeting, there was a line at the table in the back of the chapel to pick up tithing envelopes. They were going to pay their tithing.

Expect a miracle. The miracle comes.

5. *Receive the miracle with great humility.* You did not do it. The Lord did it. And the Lord will keep right on doing it with you if you get yourself in condition so He can. He wants to. We know that. Is there anyone the Lord does not want to save? He died so everyone could be saved. He wants it with all of His heart. You see, the basic missions of the Church have to do first with bring-ing souls to the Lord who are living. Second, bringing souls to the Lord that are dead. And then when you start talking about perfecting the Saints, which is the third aspect of the basic mission of the Church, I will tell you how to perfect the Saints. You get them involved in bringing souls to the Lord, living and dead. Perfecting the Saints has much to do with the first two aspects of the mission of the Church. In the process, you get per-fected automatically. That is all it takes. So the missions are all the same. It's all one mission.

Now I know it is not easy. It was never intended to be. But I also know that you can do it. You must be bold, but not overbearing. You must bridle all of your passions that you may be filled with love, and see that you refrain from idleness (See Alma 38:12). It is work, work, work and see that you are not lifted up unto pride. Yes, and see that you do not boast in your own wisdom and strength when the Lord crowns your efforts with success. Give all the credit to the Lord and He will be your constant companion and strength.

CHAPTER FIVE

Achieving Your Goals

In order to achieve goals, you must be positive. To be positive, smile, look people in the eye, shake hands firmly, be genuine, make up your mind to consistently meet your goals.

1. *Smile.* You know you have got to smile. Have you ever noticed when you give a smile you always get one back? You learned a song in Primary—"No One Likes a Frowny Face." You have got to smile. Even dogs smile. Did you ever see a dog smile? Dogs smile all the time and they get away with murder. As long as a dog is smiling, you let him climb all over you. But if he starts growling at you, (when he quits smiling), you start kicking at him. Don't you think we ought to be as smart as dogs?

I told that to a couple of Elders in Munich, Germany one time and they thought I was sort of exaggerating. "Smile?" They said, "Okay, we will try it." And so they took an old investigator's name off an "old investigator" list. Nobody had called on her, they said, for probably six or seven months. They knocked on the door. They had never met her. She came to the door. She said, "What do you want?" They did not say a word. They just smiled at her. Can you see it? I can just see those two handsome, smiling Mormon Elders. She said, "Oh, I know who you are. You are Mormon Elders. Come in." So they went right in the house. All they did was smile.

2. *Look people in the eye.* You have a spirit that is trapped in a house of clay. The only way it can see out is through these two holes right here in your head. Now the day may come when you will be able to see a lot differently than that. For now, the only thing that you can see is what you focus on. So look people in the eye and hold them with your gaze. There is a look of love you know and everybody recognizes it. Smile and look people in the eyes.

3. *Shake hands firmly.* Shake hands firmly, but gentlemanly or, you sisters, with feminine grace. It makes a difference how you shake hands. You have shaken hands with people who you feel have a limp, dead fish for a hand. You feel like you want to wipe off your hand when you get finished. There are all kinds of wild handshakes. I saw an Elder with a dislocated thumb suffered by shaking hands. Don't act foolish with outlandish kinds of handshakes. But you do need to get people by the hand firmly. Don't crush their hand, but make it sincere. It may be the only time that the person with whom you shake hands and smile and look into their face will meet a true servant of the Lord. You want it to be an experience they will never forget.

4. *Be genuine.* That means be yourself. You have got to be yourself because you cannot successfully be anyone else. Be pure, be honest, be yourself, be the best that you can be. Be a servant of the Lord.

5. *Meet your goals.* Make up your mind consistently to set and meet realistic goals, which means you must set

goals and make them high enough to require your very best efforts. Then meet your goals.

These are the steps to becoming positive. Practice these things. They will become a part of you. They will become you. And you will become the Lord's.

In the 123rd Section, verse 12, the Lord says, "For there are many yet on the earth among all sects, parties, and denominations, who are blinded by the subtle craftiness of men, whereby they lie in wait to deceive, and who are only kept from the truth because they know not where to find it." They are there. You just don't know where to look. I was one of those. I prayed one simple prayer to the Lord. If I prayed it once, I must have prayed it a thousand times. It was simply, "Dear God, please lead me to the truth. Please show me the truth." There are people all over out there, praying to the Lord that the Lord will show them the truth. And here you have it. And you are authorized to deliver it. If you do it by the spirit and with power, you will bring souls to the Lord in numbers that will astound you and your mission president and everybody else.

I had an Elder who was waiting for a visa. He was going down to Argentina. He knew the discussions well. He got up on time. He worked hard and he became a Zone leader while he was waiting for his visa. He had set his goals for that month in San Diego. Then he got his visa and left rather suddenly. I did not happen to be around at that particular moment and before I found out he was leaving, he was on the airplane and gone. He arrived down in Argentina and his new mission president was not available either. The mission president was not expecting him and was off someplace else looking after his mission. So the office staff checked with the mission president by telephone and the Elder was assigned off someplace and away he went. He said that he was not given any direction, nor any guidance. He said, "I did not know what their goals were, so I just used the goals I had in San Diego." He set his goal that he would baptize sixteen that month. And so he baptized sixteen that month. He did not know that nobody had ever baptized more than three per month in that particular area. He seemed to do quite well with a goal of sixteen, and so he set his goals a little higher next month. He said he would baptize eighteen that month, and so he baptized eighteen that month. The mission president came down and called him as an assistant. That Elder went all over the mission teaching people how to set and achieve goals.

It is so easy to do. It is so easy to bring souls to the Lord. Generally speaking, you have to ask people if they want to be baptized. You have to ask them expecting them to say yes. Have you ever asked anyone if they would like to be baptized?

I believe there is no greater time in life than when you and the Lord become one. As you go forth to bring souls to Him, you can depend on Him opening doors, preparing the way, turning their hearts to you. He will give you words to speak, thoughts to express, not only that, but He will protect you as you go. "And whoso receiveth you, there I will be also," He said, "for I will go before your face. I will be on your right hand and on your left, and my Spirit shall be in your hearts, and mine angels round about you, to bear you up" (D&C 84:88). I know He will work with you that way. He has said He would, and in the words of King Benjamin, "He never doth vary from that which he has said" (Mosiah 2:22).

I know it is true. Be positive, smile, look people in the eye, shake hands firmly, be genuine, make up your mind to consistently meet your goals. There are many of all sects who are only kept from the truth because they know not where to find it. And they will perish in unbelief if you do not bring them unto Christ. But when you bring them in, they will rise up and call you blessed for all eternity because you never forget the one who brought you the greatest gift you could have in this life—even a testimony of the Gospel of Jesus Christ and membership in the true Church and kingdom of God.

CHAPTER SIX

Using the Commitment Pattern

The method missionaries use to present the message of the restoration today is much like good missionaries have always used. It is called the commitment pattern. This procedure is a proven way to prepare the investigator to feel the Spirit of the Lord in order that the investigator might be invited to make commitments that will lead him/her into the waters of baptism. These commitments require that the investigator do the following:

1. Hear all the discussions
2. Study (particularly the Book of Mormon)
3. Pray (about what you read and hear from the missionaries)
4. Attend church (the Church of Jesus Christ of Latter-day Saints)
5. Live the Word of Wisdom (no alcohol, tobacco or tea, coffee, and drugs)
6. Pay tithes and offerings
7. Be baptized (by water and spirit)
8. Follow the living prophet

The commitment pattern requires practice in order to become skilled in using it to help the investigator achieve church membership. The commitment pattern is made up of three integral parts. They are: *prepare, invite,* and *follow-up.*

Under the preparation phase, we prepare the investigator or less-active member to feel the spirit of the Lord (since the Spirit does all the converting, meaning changing the mind and heart of the individual).This can be accomplished by teaching the investigator basic truths and preparing him/her for specific commitments. To prepare the investigator, we must build relationships of trust between the missionary and the investigator. This can be accomplished in a variety of ways as follows:

1. Be sure the missionaries keep the command-ments themselves.
2. Listen to the investigator and show empathy.
3. Answer questions by showing the answers in the scriptures.
4. Identify with the situation expressed by the investigator, perhaps by a personal experience, or an experience of someone with whom the missionary is well acquainted.
5. Show a genuine interest in the investigator.
6. Smile and look the investigator in the eye.
7. Always be nice and pleasant.

Next, we must help the investigator feel the spirit. This can be done primarily by the missionaries taking the spirit with them when they go to teach. In addition, there are a number of things that court the spirit, such as:

1. Having missionaries pray
2. Inviting investigators to pray
3. Bearing testimony
4. Identifying the spirit when it is felt by the inves-tigator. (There are times when tears fill the investigator's eyes because of the beauty of the truth the missionaries have taught. At those times, stop the discussion and tell the investiga-tor, "What you are feeling is the Holy Ghost bearing witness to the principle you have just learned.")

5. Using the scriptures, particularly the Book of Mormon
6. Committing the investigator to fast and having the missionary fast also that the investigator may over-come habits and weaknesses

When the investigator feels the spirit, then we can effectively teach the concepts. When a concept is taught, we must ask "find out" questions to see if the investigator understands the concepts, accepts the concepts, and commits to live the principles embodied in the concepts.

When the investigator feels the spirit, then we invite him/her to make a commitment. To do this we must first resolve concerns. This can be effectively done by:

1. Explaining the commitment and its ramification
2. Inviting the investigator to make the commitment
3. Expressing faith and confidence in the investigator
4. Restating the commitment
5. Accepting the commitment and confirming it
6. Listening and showing empathy
7. Expressing intentions to follow-up and help the investigator through his/her trial

Follow-up and do what you said you would do (always, always keep your word and be where you should be when you should be there).

If at any time during the teaching and inviting process the investigator or less-active member shows signs of disbelief, distrust, doubt, or confusion, the missionary must resolve concerns by going back to the preparing phase to again "build relationships of trust" and "help others feel the spirit." The teaching strategy then is: explain, demonstrate, practice, and evaluate to see how well you have taught the principles.

The only way to become competent at presenting the missionary discussions is to practice, practice, practice. In addition, a thorough knowledge of the missionary scriptures wherein you can quote them with feeling and power makes you a tremendously effective instrument in the hand of the Lord. The only way to become such a proficient servant of the Lord is to make total use of your study time provided in your daily schedule. The only way this can be done is to GET UP ON TIME. If you don't get up on time, something in your daily schedule has to give, and it's always study time that suffers. Eating never does. Make getting up on time your number one priority when you arrive in the mission field—it is the key to the success of all great missionaries.

The diagram that follows is a summary of the commitment pattern we have discussed.

COMMITMENT PATTERN

PREPARE

Prepare the investigator or less-active member to feel the Spirit. This can be accomplished by teaching them basic truths and preparing them for specific commitments. To do this we must:

1. Build Relationships of trust.
   a. Keep commandments yourself.
   b. Listen and show empathy.
   c. Use the scriptures.
   d. Identify with the situation.
   e. Use personal experiences.
   f. Be genuinely interested in them
   g. Smile and look them in the eye.
   h. Be nice.

2. Help Others to Feel the Spirit.
   a. Pray.
   b. Invite them to pray.
   c. Bear testimony.
   d. Identify the Spirit when it is felt.
   e. Use the scriptures (particularly the Book of Mormon).
   f. Fast.

3. Present the Message.
   a. Teach the concepts.

4. Find Out if the Less Active Member:
   a. Understands.
   b. Accepts.
   a. Commits.

INVITE

When less-active members feel the Spirit, then invite them to make a commitment. To do this we must:

5. Resolve Concerns.
   a. Explain the commitment.
   b. Invite to commit.
   c. Express your faith and confidence in them.
   d. Restate the commitment and listen.
   e. Accept the commitment and confirm.
   f. Listen and show empathy.
   g. Express you intention to follow up and help them.

If at any time during the teaching and inviting process the investigator or less-active member shows signs of disbelief, distrust, doubt or confusion, we must resolve their concerns by going back to the preparing phase of "Build Relationships of Trust" and "Help Others to Feel the Spirit."

FOLLOW-UP

Tell them what you are going to do to follow up which will help them to keep their commitment. Then be sure to do it!!!

(You *Must* Do
What You Say
You Will Do.)

CHAPTER SEVEN

Bringing forth the Blessings of Heaven

At this point, perhaps a discussion of bringing forth the blessings of heaven, which is the secret of "big baptismal programs," would be profitable. This information is found in the Book of Mormon, as are the answers to all others gospel questions. Alma 17:2-3 contains the secret of the success of some of the most productive missionaries who have ever lived.

Alma the younger and the sons of Mosiah had been missionaries for over fourteen years when they met by happenstance as Alma was journeying from Gideon to Manti, and the sons of Mosiah were journeying from the lands of Nephi with a host of their Lamanite converts towards Zarahemla. They were very, very, very successful missionaries—even that they had baptized thousands of converts and they had done it with true, effective, gospel principles. As Mormon records:

"And as sure as the Lord liveth, so many as were brought to the knowledge of the truth, through the preaching of Ammon and his brethren, according to the spirit of revelation and of prophecy, and the power of God working miracles in them—yea, I say unto you, as the Lord liveth, as many of the Lamanites as believed in their preaching, and were converted unto the Lord, never did fall away" (Alma 23:6). So how did they do it? The answer is in Alma 17:2-3.

> Alma did rejoice exceedingly to see his
> brethren; and what added more to his joy, they

were still his brethren in the Lord; yea, they had waxed strong in the knowledge of the truth; for they were men of a sound understanding and they had searched the scriptures diligently that they might know the word of God.

But this is not all; they had given themselves to much prayer, and fasting; therefore they had the spirit of prophecy, and the spirit of revelation, and when they taught, they taught with the power and authority of God.

The keys to their success were basically in three actions:
1. Studying the scriptures
2. Fasting
3. Praying

Let us consider these three actions separately and together.

1. *They had searched the scriptures diligently that they might know the word of God.* This means that they not only knew what the Lord had said, but they also knew where He had said it. It is vital to let the Lord tell investigators things which the missionaries cannot tell them. For instance, let us suppose that you are teaching a fine young family and you know that they (the family) know that the gospel is true, but they will not be baptized. First, you must find out why they will not do what the spirit has told them to do. This is done by asking find out questions. Suppose you find out that their parents do not want them to be baptized. Now we must resolve their concerns. We know that their parents are wrong and that

the young family should not listen to their parents in this instance. However, we cannot tell them to disobey their parents because commandment number five of the ten commandments tells them to honor their father and their mother. So we can't tell them to go against their parent's wishes, but God can tell them to follow Him and thus disobey their parents. This is, He can tell them if the missionary knows where the Lord said this.

Let's try Matt. 10:37 and let the investigators read what the Lord has said, "He that loveth father or mother more than me is not worthy of me: and he that loveth son or daughter more than me is not worthy of me." (The second half of this scripture is to handle the reverse situation where the children do not want their parents to join the church). It may be helpful at this point to show the young family what the Lord has promised to those who do follow him. "And every one that hath forsaken houses, or brethren, or sisters, or father, or mother, or wife, or children, or lands, for my name's sake shall receive an hundredfold, and shall inherit everlasting life" (Matt. 19:29). Now the young family knows what the will of the Lord is with respect to their joining the Church, so we must now make the young family sacred enough to do the Lord's will instead of their parent's will. This brings into operation the second and third actions that good missionaries must master.

2. *Fasting.* In order to make a person sacred, we must commit him/her to sacrifice. The meaning of the word sacrifice is "to make sacred." Therefore, we must commit the investigator to sacrifice. One of the easiest ways to do this is to commit the investigator to give up food and

drink for a set period of time (perhaps 24 hours). We must also give the promises of the Lord to those who do sacrifice. (I personally believe all investigators should experience fasting before they are baptized. Otherwise, the first thing that the new members experience in church is fast Sunday. If they heard nothing about fasting, they wonder what else they haven't been told which they are expected to do as members of the Church).

When the investigators commit themselves to fast, then the missionaries complement the investigators on their sincerity and commit themselves to fast with the investigators. This is very impressive to the investigators because it shows the investigators the love and sincerity of the missionaries, which is extremely important to the investigators' trust in the missionaries.

3. *Fasting must always be accompanied by the number three action, prayer.* What does the investigator pray for? The list can be very short or very long. In our example, the investigator can pray that the Lord will touch the heart of their parents or relatives who are disapproving of their baptism, or that the the family may have the courage to follow the Lord's will with respect to baptism, irrespective of their family's wishes. Or the problem with the investigator may be a Word of Wisdom problem, in which case the investigator prays for the Lord to take away the desire to smoke or drink alcohol, tea or coffee.

Whatever the problem, fasting and prayer will bring forth the blessings of heaven if the fasting and prayer is specific and sincere. One word of caution to the missionaries. You must use skill and judgment in your fasting. You can not fast every day for a week without being sent home in a box. Therefore, if you have several investigators that could profit from fasting and prayer, commit them all to fast on the same day, and then you fast once for them all. That is just as effective as fasting several times for each different investigator. Always have several investigators fasting on fast Sunday. You are going to fast that day anyway so you might as well let it be the means of helping several of your investigators to feel the spirit and help them make strong commitments.

Help each family to fast and pray for their specific needs. This is the most powerful converting principle because it courts the spirit of the Lord. Using this fasting and prayer principle has doubled the convert baptisms in every mission I have supervised since I became aware of this principle in the Book of Mormon in 1977. It worked for Alma and the sons of Mosiah, and it will surely work for you, too.

"More things are wrought by prayer (and fasting) than this world dreams of" (Idylls of the King, Alfred Lord Tennyson).

CHAPTER EIGHT

Teaching the Plan of Salvation

As the messengers of glory go forth to teach, it is necessary that they understand the message they bear. In addition, there are some basic, fundamental principles of presentation that must be followed if they are to be successful in harvesting the field. Until these principles are understood and followed, there will be but limited success, and it will almost be happenstance, bordering on luck, if anyone is baptized. The principles are as follows:

1. There is a God in Heaven and we are His children.

2. God our Father has a plan to save His children, which we call the Plan of Salvation. The Plan is based on free-agency.

3. All of God's children who are born upon this earth with a body of flesh and bone were taught the Plan, and they accepted the Plan in their pre-earth life before they were born. Those who did not accept the Plan and follow the Savior in the spirit world are not born in mortality on earth.

4. Proselyting is the process of causing one of God's children to remember the Plan (that which he/she already knows, but doesn't remember). When the missionary recalls the Plan to the investigator, it has the effect of eliminating all resistance to the true Church of God on earth.

5. The contact does not become an investigator until
   he/she commits himself/herself to study, pray, and
   attend church. In reality, it must go beyond commitment. The contact must in fact, study, pray, and attend
   church. All three of these actions are essential. No one
   or two of them is sufficient. Unless the investigator is
   willing to study the scriptures (particularly the Book of
   Mormon), prays about what he/she studies and hears
   from the missionaries, and attends the Church of Jesus
   Christ of Latter-day Saints, he/she will never become
   an investigator but will remain a contact. It is a fact
   that contacts seldom, if ever, join the Church.
   Investigators almost always join the Church.

   Many times it is impossible to get a contact to hear
   the missionary discussions. The following presentation
   could be called an overview of the Plan of Salvation. It
   does not teach the investigator everything he/she
   needs to know to be a good member of the Church,
   but it does open the door so he/she can be taught the
   gospel discussions.

6. The overview of the Plan of Salvation includes the following points, simply taught and illustrated:

   a. God is a spirit with a body of flesh and bone (true
      nature of God).
   b. We are his sons and daughters (true relationship
      to God).
   c. God loves us and wants us to be happy.
   d. We lived with God in Heaven where He taught us
      the Plan before we were born on earth.
   e. Jesus Christ has been put in charge of the Plan.
   f. The Plan is based on free agency.

g. Lucifer tried to destroy the Plan because of his greed and was cast out because of rebellion.

h. The Plan provides for us to receive a body of flesh and bone and act for ourselves. If we make mistakes, a way will be provided for us to overcome them through a Savior and Redeemer. We will provide opportunities for others to have a body of flesh and bone by having children and raising them in obedience to God's commandments. We will all die, but through our Redeemer and Savior, Jesus Christ, we will also be resurrected and live again so we can be judged and receive our reward according to our works.

i. The earth was created and the Plan was put into effect.

j. God speaks to and guides his children through special men called Prophets.

k. Prophets are necessary to teach us truths they receive from God.

l. When men follow prophets, they prosper and are happy.

m. The majority of men would not follow the prophets and thus fell into apostasy, which means refusal to follow God's prophets (which really means refusal to follow God).

n. The dispensations from Adam to Joseph Smith, each with its prophet must be represented and explained.

o. The place of Gordon B. Hinckley, the living prophet, is explained.

p. An appointment is made to return and tell in detail how the gospel was restored in this dispensation (including the Joseph Smith testimony, which includes the visit of Moroni and the presentation of the Book of Mormon with a commitment to read the book).

If we teach by the spirit and use information which

the investigator previously knew, almost all resistance to the proselyting discussions is eliminated. It is in the proselyting discussions that the material presented in the overview of the Plan of Salvation is enlarged and ampli- fied. Also there is little resistance to the overview presen- tation, which means the teaching of the discussions can move along much faster and much more effectively. This is true primarily because the pieces have already been fit together and the discussions now amplify and show how the principles of the gospel apply in the lives of the investigator.

When the missionary observes the Holy Ghost bear- ing witness to the investigator, the elder or sister then makes the investigator aware of the testimony he/she is receiving. This procedure is plainly taught in numerous places in the Book of Mormon. In the 18th chapter of Alma, Ammon gained the confidence of King Lamoni by defending his flocks and chopping off the arms of his attackers. King Lamoni asked to talk to Ammon. Ammon began by asking the King if he believed there is a God.

> "And he answered, and said unto him: I do not know what that meaneth.
> "And then Ammon said: Believest thou that there is a Great Spirit?
> "And he said, Yea.
> "And Ammon said: This is God. And Ammon said unto him again: Believest thou that this Great Spirit, who is God, created all things which are in heaven and in the earth?
> "And he said: Yea, I believe that he created all things which are in the earth; but I do not know the heavens.

"And Ammon said unto him: The heavens is a place where God dwells and all his holy angels too.

"And king Lamoni said: Is it above the earth?

"And Ammon said: Yea, and he looketh down upon all the children of men; and he knows all the thoughts and intents of the heart; for by his hand were they all created from the beginning.

"And king Lamoni said: I believe all these things which thou hast spoken. Art thou sent from God?

Ammon said unto him: I am a man; and man in the beginning was created after the image of God, and I am called by his Holy Spirit to teach these things unto this people, that they may be brought to a knowledge of that which is just and true.

And a portion of that Spirit dwelleth in men, which giveth me knowledge, and also power according to my faith and desires which are in God.

Now when Ammon had said these words, he began at the creation of the world, and also the creation of Adam, and told all the things concerning the fall of man, and rehearsed and laid before him the records and the holy scriptures of the people, which had been spoken by the prophets, even down to the time that their father, Lehi, left Jerusalem" (Alma 18: 25-36).

In our day, we would rehearse through Joseph Smith and Gordon B. Hinckley. Then verse 39 says:

"But this is not all; for he expounded unto them the plan of redemption, which was prepared from the foundation of the world; and he also made known unto them concerning the coming of Christ, and all the works of the Lord did he make known unto them."

This today would relate to the proselyting discussion. This method of teaching was effective then, and it is effective now. The same procedure was followed by Aaron with king Lamoni's father in the land of Nephi as recorded in the 22nd chapter of Alma:

> "And it came to pass that when Aaron saw that the king would believe his words, he began from the creation of Adam, reading the scriptures unto the king—how God created man after his own image, and that God gave him commandments, and that because of transgression, man had fallen.
> "And Aaron did expound unto him the scriptures for the creation of Adam, laying the fall of man before him, and their carnal state and also the plan of redemption, which was prepared from the foundation of the world, through Christ, for all whosoever would believe on his name.
> "And since man had fallen he could not merit anything of himself; but the sufferings and death of Christ atone for their sins, through faith and repentance, and so forth; and that he breaketh the bands of death, that the grave shall have no victory; and that the sting of death should be swallowed up in the hopes of glory; and Aaron did expound all these things unto the king.
> And it came to pass that after Aaron had expounded these things unto him, the king said: What shall I do that I may have this eternal life of which thou hast spoken?" (Alma 22:12-15)

This method of teaching was tremendously effective and the converts had great staying power.

> "Behold, now it came to pass that the king of the Lamanites sent a proclamation among all his

people, that they should not lay their hands on Ammon, or Aaron, or Omner, or Himni, nor either of their brethren who should go forth preaching the word of God, in whatsoever place they should be, in any part of their land.

"And now it came to pass that when the king had sent forth this proclamation, that Aaron and his brethren went forth from city to city, and from one house of worship to another, establishing churches, and consecrating priests and teachers throughout the land among the Lamanites, to preach and to teach the word of God among them; and thus they began to have great success.

"And thousands were brought to the knowledge of the Lord, yea, thousands were brought to believe in the traditions of the Nephites; and they were taught the records and prophecies which were handed down even to the present time.

"And as sure as the Lord liveth, so sure as many as believed, or as many as were brought to the knowledge of the truth, through the preaching of Ammon and his brethren, according to the spirit of revelation and of prophecy, and the power of God working miracles in them—yea, I say unto you, as the Lord liveth, as many of the Lamanites as believed in their preaching, and were converted unto the Lord never did fall away" (Alma 23:1, 4-6).

I am convinced that when this approach is followed today, the same results will be obtained. Therefore, I am presenting a sample presentation that could be used to prepare the way for the standard proselyting discussions, only when the standard discussions cannot be presented.

Missionary: Mr. Brown, it is a pleasure for us to be with you and your family. It gives us the opportunity to tell you that we know that God lives, that

Jesus is the Christ and that the Church of Jesus
Christ of Latter-day Saints is the kingdom of God on
earth. We testify that the true Church is on earth
because our Father in Heaven loves His children
and wants to bless us through the activities of His
church. We would like to answer three questions for
you. 1), Where did I come from? 2), Why am I here?
3), Where am I going after this life is over?

In order to understand the first question, we
must know that before we were born into this life,
we lived in what is known as the pre-earth existence, or premortal existence. Every person to be
born on this earth lived in this premortal existence.
We had a Heavenly Father and Mother. We did not
have physical bodies of flesh and bone as we now
have. We lived as spirits—children of our Heavenly
Father. A spirit, Mr. Brown, is a personage, and has
the same form as a mortal person but does not have
flesh and bones. As spirits, we were able to commu-
nicate, move about, make decisions and choices and
recognize the difference between good and evil.
God our Heavenly Father is not merely a spirit, but
has a body of flesh and bone which is tangible, like
man's, though it is glorified and perfected.

As His spirit children, we could see in our premortal existence that our Heavenly Father had a
glorified body of flesh and bones, which was necessary to progress eternally, and we desired to be like
him. Because of his love for us, he prepared a way
for us to obtain physical bodies like His. This plan
required that we obtain these physical bodies by
coming to this earth to live. Let's talk for a moment
about the importance of having this physical body.
God is a God of love, and seeks that which is best
for each of us. Therefore, He provided a plan for us,
which we call the plan of salvation, so we could
become more like him. To gain wisdom like God
has, we needed many experiences, particularly since

there are many things we could not learn or do as a spirit in the premortal life. For example, a spirit cannot feel physical pain or suffering and learn by experience what pain is. Neither can a spirit be baptized or married, nor experience the pain and joy of having children. To obtain experiences like these, we had to come to this earth and receive physical bodies.

A second reason we came to this earth was to develop faith in God. Our Heavenly Father wants all of his children to have faith in him. Obviously if we have faith in him, we must learn to trust him and have confidence in His promises to us. In our premortal existence, we walked primarily by sight. In this earth life, we walk primarily by faith. Our Heavenly Father made it possible for us to live by faith by making us forget the premortal life. Therefore, we live not by memory, but by faith, which is belief plus action. Then God tests our faith to see if we will keep all His commandments when we are not in His presence. Some of these commandments are: to believe in God and have faith in Him, repent of our sins, be baptized, and love and serve one another. God measures our love and faith in Him by how well we keep the commandments. He told his disciples, if ye love me, keep my commandments. As we keep His commandments, our faith grows, and we prepare to live with our Heavenly Father in His kingdom. No one can ever be saved in His kingdom without showing faith by obeying the Lord's commandments. Neither can we be truly happy without keeping His commandments.

So that we will have our Heavenly Father's guidance and direction, God has sent special men to the earth who talk with God and teach us what God wants us to do so we can be happy. These special men are called Prophets. They talk with God and

God talks with them. Then they give the message to the people. (Put this information on the drawing you are going to leave with the investigator–see drawing on page 82). Prophets are very, very, important. Do you know who the first prophet was? That's right, it was the first man—Adam. (Write ADAM and 1st man in upper left hand side of the page–see diagram on page 82). God spoke to Adam and his wife Eve in the Garden of Eden and gave them commandments, which they broke. So they had to leave the Garden. When they left the Garden of Eden, they became mortal and began to bear children. But the spirits that gave their children life came from heaven. We lived with God the Father awaiting our turn on earth. Adam and Eve had many children. Two of their very famous children were Cain and Abel. Abel was a good son because he followed the Prophet Adam, who was also his father. But Cain was rebellious and wicked and killed his brother Abel. This started the first apostasy. (Draw a line down to the bottom of the paper and write the world APOSTASY.)

Do you know what that means, Mr. Brown? Yes, that means that the people refused to follow the Lord's prophet and thus lost contact with God and fell into a state of spiritual darkness, ignorance, disobedience, and iniquity. This is called apostasy. After Adam's time, the bulk of the people were in apostasy for hundreds of years. This is not to say they weren't religious. They were. They had lots of churches. They worshiped the sun, the rain, the moon, rocks, mountains, etc. But did they have the truth? No, they did not. The people became so bad that God decided that the only solution was to destroy them all with a great flood—cleanse the earth—and start over. But before He destroyed the earth, God sent a special prophet whose name was Noah. Noah walked and talked with God face to face as one man speaketh to another, just as Adam had, but the people wouldn't listen. So God had Noah build an ark to save his family. (Write the name NOAH at the top of the paper opposite ADAM and draw the ark.)

After the flood, Noah's family lived together happily for a while and they kept the Lord's commandments and began to re-populate the earth. Much later, Noah's descendants began to build cities like Sodom and Gomorrah. Mr. Brown, what were the people like in these cities? That's right, they were extremely wicked, primarily because they refused to follow the Prophet which God sent to tell them to repent. (Draw the line back down to the APOSTASY.) God sent another prophet, Abraham. (Write the name ABRAHAM opposite ADAM and NOAH). Abraham walked and talked to God face to face as one man speaks to another. Because the people in Sodom and Gomorrah refused to listen to the Prophet Abraham, they were in a state of apostasy. What were they doing? They were drinking, smoking, using drugs, being immoral, committing fornication and adultery. What did the Prophet tell them to do? To repent, or stop doing these things, and be baptized for a remission of their sins and live so the spirit could guide them. When they rejected the words of God's prophet, God rained down fire and brimstone and destroyed the cities and everyone in them. (Draw the smoke curling up from Sodom and Gomorrah.)

Mr. Brown, do you think people who live in a state of apostasy could be happy? Obviously not, but because God loves his children and wants them to be happy, He gave them the Prophet Abraham to bring them up out of apostasy. God really tested Abraham to see how much faith he had. Do you remember in the Bible how God told Abraham to offer his son, Isaac, as a burnt offering? Abraham took his son and went up on the mountain and was about to slay his son when an angel appeared and told Abraham not to sacrifice his son, that he had shown his faith in God. Abraham became a great prophet and led the people in righteousness, but there were many that began to say: "If I had lived in the time of Noah, I would have followed him. I would have been on the ark with him, but this crazy guy Abraham, he tells me that I have to repent and be baptized. I don't even have any sins to repent of. I'm not going to follow him." What do you think, Mr. Brown? Do you think the people that rejected the living Prophet Abraham would have followed Noah and been on the ark with Noah and his family? Probably not—because when the people reject the words of a living prophet, they are really rejecting the words of who? That's right—GOD. And if the people rejected God's words at the time of Abraham, they would have rejected Noah also.

What happened to these people was a repeat of what had happened before—they gradually fell back down into another apostasy. (Draw a line back down to the APOSTASY.) And what does that mean? That's right—they refused to follow God's prophets and once again began to do things, such as committing adultery and fornication, using harmful drugs, teaching false doctrines, etc. that caused them to lose the Spirit of the Lord. Mr. Brown, do you think these people who again fell into apostasy were really happy? No—that's right. They couldn't be happy, could they? They no longer followed the will of our Heavenly Father, and so suffered the consequences of His punishment. As you remember, they fell into the hands of the Egyptians and became their slaves for 360 years. (Draw chains on the paper and ask Mr. Brown what they are.) That's right, Mr. Brown, these are chains. Mr. Brown, these people were not only chained to the Egyptians.

They were also chained to unhappiness. They were in bondage for many hundreds of years until our Heavenly Father saw it was necessary to help these people (His children) once again.

Mr. Brown, considering what our Heavenly Father did in the past when his children needed help (point to the illustration where the prophets are), what do you think He did to free these people that were in bondage? He called another what? That's right, another prophet. These people who were in apostasy were religious. They were worshipping all kinds of things which they had picked up from the Egyptians—the worship of physical things, such as water, sun, moon, clouds, rocks, and graven images. However, they did not have the truth because they did not have a prophet. So our Heavenly Father gave them a prophet to free them from bondage. What was his name? That's right, his name was Moses. (Write MOSES' name opposite the previous prophets.) Moses was a great prophet for he walked and talked with God face to face as one man speaketh to another. Moses not only freed the children of Israel from bondage, but once more their hearts were free to follow God through his living prophet Moses. Moses led the children of Israel to the Red Sea with Pharaoh's army following after to kill them. Moses was trapped with the Red Sea on one side and pharaoh's army on the other. So what did he do? That's right, he separated or parted the water, and those that followed Moses and the Lord passed through the Red Sea on dry ground. But what happened to pharaoh's army when they tried to pass through? Yes. They were drowned, weren't they? So obviously those who followed the living Prophet Moses were much happier than those who didn't. These people became a very happy people. They were no longer in bondage and did not have that hardship anymore. They showed their love for

God by following the Prophet Moses, and God showed his love for them by giving them direction and guidance through His prophet Moses.

Moses led the people to Mt. Sinai, and there he left them for a season while he went up into the mountain as God had commanded him to do and there received the ten commandments. Moses was overjoyed and excited to share these commandments with his people, but when Moses came down from the mountain, he found his people, the children of Israel, worshipping a golden calf. They were also being immoral, and no doubt using harmful drugs. Mr. Brown, do you think this is what God had told Moses to have the people do? No, indeed, God is a jealous God and He wants his children to worship him only. What happened to these people while Moses was gone? That's right, they had fallen into apostasy. (Draw a line back down to APOSTASY.) They had begun to follow the ideas of man and not of God. Sure they were religious—they were worshipping an idol—a golden calf—but they had rejected the living Prophet Moses and were in apostasy. And apostasy means they either have no prophet, or they refuse to follow their prophet. Mr. Brown, do you think these people were happy in their apostasy? Because they didn't follow the prophet, they had to follow their own wisdom, which is always foolishness to God. How much easier it would have been if they had just followed Moses.

These people were in a state of apostasy for many hundreds of years until Heavenly Father, out of his great love for His children, sent his son Jesus Christ to restore the truth that the people had lost when they rejected Moses. As we learned earlier, Jesus was to be born upon the earth as the literal son of God and was to take upon himself the sins of all men, and make immortality and eternal life available to all God's children. Mr. Brown, do you believe in Jesus Christ? Good. (Write JESUS CHRIST on the paper.) Mr. Brown, I want you to know that I know that Jesus Christ is literally the Son of God the Father and that He was born upon the earth, and that He did take upon himself the sins of all men, on condition of their repentance. I also know that He was crucified upon the cross, and that He rose from the dead on the third day and was seen by many. Mr. Brown, I bear witness that Jesus is the Christ and that He does live today.

Mr. Brown, do you think Jesus followed any of the different religions that were here upon the earth when He was here? As you remember, these people were very religious—they worshiped idols, the suns, stars, moon, etc., but did they have all the truth? No. That is why Jesus didn't follow any of these other churches. Instead, He established on the earth the true Church of Jesus Christ. In addition, Christ did many marvelous things for the people. He healed the sick, raised the dead, and taught the people the true gospel, which included having faith in him, repenting of their sins, and being baptized with water and with fire and the Holy Ghost. Jesus Christ chose twelve special witnesses and ordained them by the laying on of His hands, which gave them authority to act for him. He sent them out to preach his gospel and baptize all those who were willing to repent and follow Him. As Jesus Christ and his apostles preached these things (just like Adam, Noah, Abraham and Moses did), the people rejected their message. They said, just as those before them had, "We will follow all the prophets up to and including Moses. In fact, if we had lived in the times of Moses, we would have followed him, but this Jesus, he tells us to repent and be baptized and follow him. He is crazy. He is teaching all these crazy things. Who is he anyway—just a carpenter's son." (see Matt 13:55-56)

In the end, Mr. Brown, what did the people do to Jesus? That's right, they crucified him. They rejected the word of God by killing God's son, Jesus. And after they had killed Him, they fell into another apostasy. (Draw another line down to the APOSTA-SY.) They went through the dark ages and didn't progress spiritually for hundreds and hundreds of years. How much easier it would have been if they had only followed the Lord Jesus Christ and repented of their sins and been baptized for the remission of their sins in the name of Jesus Christ.

Of course, these people in apostasy were very religious. There were a lot of different churches here on earth, but none of them had a living prophet, which means they had no guidance from God, only the wisdom of men. They did remember Jesus and so they used the cross (draw a cross on the paper) as a sign of Christianity, but they made many changes in His teachings. What did the Romans use to crucify Jesus? That's right, a cross. (Point to the cross on the paper.) Then really, Mr. Brown, the cross is a sign of what? (Point to the word APOSTASY.)

Mr. Brown, these people were in apostasy for hundred and hundreds of years until our Heavenly Father once again restored his true Church to earth again. To do this, Mr. Brown, God called another what? Right. A prophet. Mr. Brown, that is the importance of our message to you today, that God has not left us here alone today. Because of God's great love for us, He called another Prophet. His name was Joseph Smith. I bear testimony in the name of Jesus Christ that Joseph Smith was a true prophet of God. Let me tell you a little bit about Joseph Smith. (Tell the Joseph Smith Story as it stands in the discussions.)

Mr. Brown, God and Jesus Christ spoke to whom? (Point to Joseph Smith.) And what do we call men who talk to God? (Point to all of the prophets.) So what was Joseph Smith? Right, a prophet who walked and talked with God face to face as one man speaketh to another. (Here missionary bears testimony of Joseph Smith and points out the witness of the Holy Ghost that he knows that Joseph Smith was a prophet.)

Mr. Brown, ever since Joseph Smith, there has always been a prophet on earth and there is today. Our Heavenly Father has promised us that if we do not follow the living prophet on earth today, we will fall into another apostasy. The way He keeps us from doing this is He keeps a living prophet upon the earth to give us guidance from God to help us to prepare for the second coming of Jesus Christ. Mr. Brown, that is the reason there is a prophet today. His name is Gordon B. Hinckley. (Write GORDON B. HINCKLEY on the paper on the prophet line.) He is a living prophet of God. Mr. Brown, just as you know that Joseph Smith was a Prophet because of the Holy Ghost, also know the Holy Ghost is telling you that Gordon B. Hinckley is a prophet of God.

Mr. Brown, we can be like all the people in the past who said it was too hard to repent and be baptized and who rejected the living prophet. Or, we can show our faith in God and follow His living prophets today. Mr. Brown, would you like to receive the blessings of love and harmony and the real joy and happiness in your life through the satisfaction that comes from following God's living prophet? Mr. Brown, we bear testimony that these blessings will be yours as you follow the prophet of God. (Here the missionaries make an appointment to return within two days to instruct Mr. Brown further in how he can prepare himself to receive the blessings of membership in Jesus Christ's true church).

It may seem at first exposure that this lesson moves too fast into the heart of the message of the restoration. However, experience has demonstrated that this overview of the Plan of Salvation is a tremendously solid foundation to support the truths contained in the proselyting discussions. Coupled with the seven principles of conversion, those who continue beyond an overview of the plan of salvation, will invariably be baptized and become members of the Church.*

> *NOTE: The drawing that has been completed as the lesson progressed is left with Mr. Brown and used in subsequent discussions. Also a copy of Joseph Smith's Testimony is also left with the investigator with encouragement to read it, ponder it, and pray about it that his/her understanding may increase and his/her testimony may grow.

The overview of the Plan of Salvation then prepares the way for the six proselyting discussions which must be presented before the investigator is prepared for baptism. In addition, the investigator must attend church, meet the Bishop or Branch President and be interviewed by a full-time missionary before he/she is recommended for baptism and is then baptized.

After baptism and before the closing prayer, the new convert should be greeted by a ward family history consultant and presented a special "Legacy of Love" packet containing family group sheets and pedigree charts with a brief explanation of what they are. An appointment is set to get the new convert prepared to attend the temple within thirty to sixty days to do baptisms and confirmations for their kindred dead.

The discussions for new members are taught by the Stake missionaries and the new converts' names are placed upon the convert baptismal check-list with a view of making them fellow citizens with the Saints and providing them with all the preparation needed to have them sealed in the temple by the end of one year of church membership (if they are married). We really baptize people then so they can go to the temple and begin the road to eternal life–which is the object and design of our existence.

That we might all become involved in this grand endeavor is the work and glory of our Heavenly Father and His grand design for all His children (see Moses 1:39). This all begins with baptism because God our Heavenly Father has no salvation for His children outside of the House of Israel of which we become part when we are baptized and confirmed a member of the church. Therefore, let the teaching and baptizing roll forth with ever increasing momentum.

Much love,

Hartman Rector, Jr.

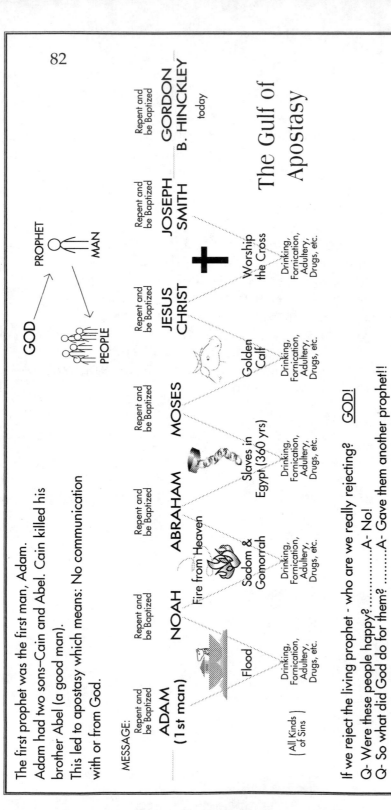

The first prophet was the first man, Adam.
Adam had two sons—Cain and Abel. Cain killed his brother Abel (a good man).
This led to apostasy which means: No communication with or from God.

MESSAGE:

GOD → PROPHET → MAN / PEOPLE

| ADAM (1st man) | NOAH | ABRAHAM | MOSES | JESUS CHRIST | JOSEPH SMITH | GORDON B. HINCKLEY (today) |

Repent and be Baptized (under each prophet)

Flood — Fire from Heaven — Sodom & Gomorrah — Slaves in Egypt (360 yrs) — Golden Calf — Worship the Cross

(All Kinds of Sins) — Drinking, Fornication, Adultery, Drugs, etc.

The Gulf of Apostasy

If we reject the living prophet - who are we really rejecting?   GOD!

Q- Were these people happy?...........A- No!
Q- So what did God do for them? ....A- Gave them another prophet!!

THE ONLY WAY TO GET TO HEAVEN IS TO FOLLOW THE LIVING PROPHET!!

The people in apostasy always said, "If we had lived in the days of the dead prophets—we would have followed them." But they would not follow the living prophet.